The Color of Love

BY RAYMOND QUATTLEBAUM

AuthorHouse™
1663 Liberty Drive
Bloomington, IN 47403
www.authorhouse.com
Phone: 1 (800) 839-8640

Published by AuthorHouse 07/13/2018

ISBN: 978-1-5462-3117-2 (sc)
ISBN: 978-1-5462-3118-9 (e)

authorHOUSE®

Table of Contents

INTRODUCTION

<u>The Color Of Love!</u>

Beauty is the color of Happiness.
Happiness is the color of Love.
Love Is The Color Of Life.
Life is the color of God, in it's highest form.
Love is the color of life, in it's creation.
So love colors itself in the form of life.
The color of love is life, Heavenly Beautiful.
God is all love Inevitably Beautiful.
we are God's love in the form of creation.
The presence of God is who we truly are within ourselves.
Multidimensional Beauty is the landscape of life,
the Divine presence of God.
Heavenly, Beautiful, is The Breath Of Life.
Here is a book materialized into love.
Magnificently, Unbelievable.
Yes! Absolutely, Amazing.
Because love makes the world go around.
All things evolve from love, and blossoms from it.
Love is the existence of all life.
We live and breath through God's Divine Love.
It is all around us in it's infinite form.
The Divine presence of God. Miraculously, Beautiful.
And so we dance to a creation called life.
A Spectrum of Mulitdimensional Infinite Beauty.
The Color Of Love. An array of Infinite Affection.
An absolute miracle in the arms of God.
Divine, Love, forever, Beautiful. The Color Of Love.
The Spectrum Of Life!!!

Magnificence!

All greatness comes from God.
A mathematical equation some find hard.
The manifestation of who we are,
The composition of a star.
The Miracle life from a far,
do you know who you are.
Even though we stand tall,
the beauty of life starts off small.
Infinite greatness reigns through us all,
This is the truth God recalls.
Recognizing the essence of who you are,
divine reality takes you far.
Like the brilliance of a star,
this is the concept of who you are.
Breaking down the Essence from the beginning of time.
We are the products of God's infinite mind.
Feel the power of his Divine,
a reflection of love with an Infinite shine.
This is the beauty of God's mind,
believe the power of your mind.
God's infinite greatness comes with time.
Yours is one with an Infinite shine.
A mathematical equation you will find,
You are the offspring of a beautiful mind.
The manufacturer of life is God's design.
The manifestation of life is a star,
the transformation of life is who you are.

By-Raymond Quattlebaum AKA-Ray Q

A Race!

A race so powerful,
so inspiring,
so uplifting,
born with universal
strength. Melanized
through the materialization
of birth. Melanin is
their first name,
backed by popular demand.
A force to be reckon with,
the force of one, thee one,
they are the one. A race,
oppressed, suppressed.
and depressed,
feeling life's atrocities.
Painstaking to the core,
life's greatest hardships,
excruciating to their souls.
The hardships of life.
A race on the frontier line
of life's battleground,
holding down the ground.
No battle could've prepared
them more, in a battle
to the end.
A race who've been broken down
in content to morning, afternoon,
and evening, but they are the night.
A race destine to prevail,
for victory is mine.
A race hated for the entities
they are, but loved for the
performances of their souls.
A race responsible for spi-
ritual awareness, life's
righteousness, detoured from
their original path. A race
stripped of their trophies
of achievement, prized pos-
sessions, stripped butt naked.

Shot down as degenerates,
but they are truly Gods.
A race racing to recapture the
true dignity of their pride,
and soul. A race marinated
within its source strength,
for they are true strength.
A race marked by the color of
their skin, but black is the
beginning of everything, life's
darkest treasures.
A race, feel me, as I cry out
to you. For we are, who we are,
and what we are. We are the
true shadow of darkness. We
are the legendary Black Race.
The darkest treasure of them
all, life's everlasting begin-
ning. Feel me!!!

By-Raymond Quattlebaum
A.K.A.-Ray Q

A Rainbow Colors The Sky

Why ashamed!
Why should anyone be ashame,
for who they are.
we are all reflections
of the most high,
in his infinite glory.
The beautiful colors,
that are in the world,
a true essence, a rainbow.
A coalition of astonishing
colors high in it's spiritual guidance.
From the beginning, and never ends.
Color me beautiful,
you are as beautiful as your thoughts.
Color my world.
In the form of unconditional love.
Radiating from all endeavors of creation.
The colors of emotion, the seen, and unseen.
The high, and the low, permeating life,
throughout the galaxies. Dimensional Love.
Like an artist paints a picture.
On all levels of creation,
simply astonishing.
Like the configuration of a snowflake,
rare, and unique, in it's own beauty.
Like no other beauty.
God is forever Beautiful!

By-Raymond Quattlebaum_AKA-Ray Q

Are We All The Same

Is there a season for some reason,
cause I feel the pain.
They're killing us off one, by one,
so who's gonna take the blame.
I sit here and ask myself,
are we all the same.
If right was wrong and wrong was right,
would there be a light.
Take a look at what their doing,
they're heading for a fight.
They shoot us down right in the streets,
and tell their dog's to bite,
now this confuses you and me,
but to them it's just alright.
I ask myself, are we all the same,
something for us to think about, we
better call God's name.
Because their playing a dangerous game,
now who's gonna take the blame.
Why should we be ashamed, or even feel
this pain, just because we have black
skin, their aiming to destroy us again.
Yeah! The land of the brave and free,
but black is not suppose to be!
AND THEY SAY WERE FREE!!!
Apparently, nobody wants to see,
just how could this be.
You would think they got us trained,
if they had a chance to do it all over
again, they would put us back in chains.
They pat you on your back, shake your
hand, and say you are my friend.
In all reality what they're doing is
playing you to the end.
This is something some won't see,
because we say love is blind.
If you don't know the truth by now,
you better check the time.
Every time I read the paper a brother
is going down, we're living in dangerous
times today, HEY!! you better look around.
HATE! Is in the atmosphere and this is
how it sounds, PA, PA, PA, PA,
is what you hear, a black man hits the ground,
what a familiar sound. There's nothing to be
said, the brother is already dead.
So who's gonna take the blame? Now ask
yourself!
Are we all the same, we're living in deadly pain.
Should we take the blame, we better call god's
name, because we are not the same.
Cause their playing a deadly game!!!!!!

By-Raymond Quattlebaum-AKA-Ray Q

Am I Dreaming

We are more than just
the flesh, we are the
offsprings of a greater reality.

I have lived realities,
and realities.
Realities who are me.
My spiritual essence,
allows me to see.

All these replicas
images of me,
the only real time
I could ever be free.

I returned to All That There Is To Be!
In his presence,
beautiful music is what I hear,
sounds of music
playing everywhere.

Celestial beings
I don't even know,
family members I guess so.
And this unbelievable feeling
I couldn't explain,

Why like colors of spiritual rain.
These incredible colors
in front of my eyes,
it took my breath away,
I wouldn't lie.

A feeling came over me,
I knew I could fly.
A beautiful feeling, a spiritual high.
Then in one minute,
as I recalled.

I had the knowledge of it all.
Then I had to go back to Earth,
start a new life,
but come back through birth.

As unbelievable as it may have seemed,
this experience wasn't a dream.
Who would ever think death
would be so grand,
cordially invited to meet the Man!

By-Raymond Quattlebaum-A.K.A.-Ray Q
8/27/01

Are You My Brother!

It's a shame how some people walk around
portraying to be down.
society has no room for ignorance,
therefore, you are down. Yes! so down no one
sees you. You walk around with a ice face grill,
like the world is at your kill.
Brother I feel your pain, it's been around for years,
the raining season is your tears.
Ignorance real name should be fear,
this is how he gets his scare.
So you go around boasting I am a man,
but destroying the next brother anyway you can.
This is not the measure of a man,
his true nature is to stand.
The sad part is you believe you got people shook,
brother ignorance has really got you hooked.
open up your eyes my brother look! the key to life is a book.
Education! What! that's not for me,
education brother is your reality, the future is made for
you to see. This is why you can't be free.
There are things you need to know,
education will help you grow. It's imperative that you know,
your true strength will begin to show.
Then your world will begin to grow.
Knowledge is Power! this is how you go!
Let no one tell you No! your true essence will begin to show.
Tell the brothers what you know!
You don't have to express yourself by saying YO!
this is how you begin to grow.
Knowledge is Power! Brother, know you know!!!

Baby Girl!

Trapped off in the world
and that's not to kool.
Because baby girl has never
completed school.
Without a shadow of a doubt,
drugs and ignorance,
has turned her out.
And it's so sad because of school,
baby girl has been played for a fool.
Most people think she's slow,
disrespected, and neglected,
looked upon as a hoe.
Baby girl has reached her bottom
with no place to go.
It's a frightning situation,
her parents don't even know.
She's been trampled on, kicked, even
pushed to the side, baby girls
only resort was to breakdown and cry.
It even crossed her mind one day,
she sat down and said why?
I can't tell a lie.
All the knowledge in the world,
is it worth a high.
Millions of opportunities will come about,
but they will always pass her by.
It's such a devastating result,
no matter how hard she tries.
I thought I was all that, even without school,
people started to play me out,
use me as a fool.
I thought hanging out,
and getting high made me look kool.
Now my life is not so well.
I can't even read or write,
not so much as spell.
Baby girl, you mean to tell me,
you couldn't tell?
How I wish I went to school,
my life's a living Hell!

Baby girl, Dahhhhh!! Hello!!!
You know Education rings a Bell.
Wooooooow! A mind is a terrible thing to waste,
baby girl it's not hard to tell!!!!

By-Raymond Quattlebaum-AKA-Ray Q

Baby

Baby Keep Me Comong

I'll wash your body baby, you'll wash mine.
Heavenly love is heavenly fine.
Beautiful love is so Divine.
lets not even consider the time,
baby now you know whats on my mind.

Baby Keep Me Coming

I'll kiss your body baby, and hold you tight,
our love's burning like a burning light.
Heavenly love feels so heavenly right.
Baby lets make love all through the night.

Baby Keep Me Coming

The fire burning in our hearts,
our love is playing a sexual part. We look into each
others eyes, full of wonder and surprise.
Making heavenly love within our souls, baby
I feel the love within my toes.

Baby Keep Me Coming

I run my fingers through your hair, you scream out,
Honey! Baby! Yes! My Dear! the color of love is everywhere,
this is love sexually clear, a vision of a spiral stair.
Ascending love throughout the air, this is love heavenly clear.

Baby Keep Me Coming

As we pump each other ever so lovely, feeling a sexual rain,
a feeling like we heavenly came.
A feeling which we both can claim.
A screaming desire anticipating more, a sexual desire
we both adore.

Baby Keep Me Coming

Riding on the waves of our love. As we lay butt naked
on the floor, no love could have loved us more.
Baby our love's like a Candy Store, honey you wanna hear
this lion roar Baby this is love forevermore.
Heavenly, Love, to the core. This is why we are on the floor.
Baby Keep Me Coming Back For more, and more, and more,
and forevermore, more!!! Baby Keep Me Coming!!!!!

Can We Find The Truth

Some people travel around the world,
inquiring about the truth.
God, says, time is of the essence today,
teach it to our youth.

Others say, the time is now, and history
has the proof. Skeptics, of a different
sound, laughing it off as a goof.
Scientist, of the world today, telling
Historians to boof.

Escavations in the ground finding relics loose.
Anthropologist, who are renown,
searching for the truth.
Ancient artifacts that were found, that are human
tooth.

Geologist, there are findings in the ground, and
we have the proof. This is where it was found,
I'm telling you the truth.

Historians, I keep coming up with these words,
can we find the truth. The answer is here,
to be found, enlighten our youth, this is how
it comes around, and history has the proof.

Anthropologist, the digging that was in the
ground,
something came up loose.
Skeptics, I don't believe a word they say,
now take that stuff and boof.

Scientist, we're the genius of the world,
evidently, you guys don't have any proof.
Geologist, so you don't believe a word we say,
and you think we don't have any proof.

Historians, then how do you explain the proven
fact, they found a two million year old human
tooth.

Skeptics, what is this, some kind of game, your
trying to teach the youth.

Anthropologist, listen, we keep coming up with
these words,
is there anybody out there listening?
Can we find the truth!!!

By-Raymond Quattlebaum-AKA-Ray Q
8/13/01

Change!

Everything in life is subject to change.
From the smallest, to the Infinite.
As there is so High, there is so Below.
There is no life without change,
and no change without life.
Change is the only true sacrafice.
In order to grow you must change,
the representation of change is growth.
the greatest perception of change is life.
The only thing in life that's constant is change.
The circulation of life doesn't remain the same,
the rotation of life brings about change.
The word change grows so far,
the reflection of change shows who you are.
The past lives we lived awe! that's just not true,
the changes we lived it's all about you.
Change, the manifestation of what we will be,
change is expressing itself from you to me.
So you don't want to change,
then there's no future to see.
As I lay in the shadow for the next day to come,
change brought about the morning and sun.
And darkness not leaving a trace for no one to see,
change is the coloration of space to me.
As we work on ourselves everyday to make our lives shine,
change is renting space in our state of mind.
Change, the corporation of infinite time,
you either manifest, or fall behind.
Change, more powerful than the eyes can see,
change are the thoughts from you to me.
Change, transforms itself once more again,
when one door closes, another one begins.
Change, is destine for you to win.
Absolutely, Remarkable, why we even change to take off our
clothes. You must remember,
you are the masters of your being.
Masters of your growth. Masters of your existence.
You have free will, it's up to you to make a change.
You are the creators of your own creation.
You see! Life is not something that's far out of range,
in order to be in life, you must materialize,
CHANGE!!!

By-Raymond Quattlebaum-AKA-Ray Q

Find A Way

My heart shines with happiness,
therefore, happiness shines with love.

If your sad, upset, feeling sorrow,
things will always come tomorrow.
<u>LOVE WILL FIND THE WAY!</u>

Don't let blues get you down, you
know love comes around.
<u>LOVE WILL FIND THE WAY!</u>

Due away with that frown, you can't
live upside down, evidently, love
will be found.
<u>LOVE WILL FIND THE WAY!</u>

Though you do, what you do, good
times will pull you through for-
<u>LOVE WILL FIND THE WAY!</u>

So your mad extremely confused, just
about to blow your fuse!
Sit back, take a deep breath, don't
let your anger be the ref, cause-
<u>LOVE WILL FIND THE WAY!</u>

Emotions got you in a spin, be real
kool love will win.
This is how it all begins,
<u>LOVE WILL FIND THE WAY!</u>

Broken heart, heart aches again,
those are love desires burning within,
love is design for you to win, absolutely-
<u>LOVE WILL FIND THE WAY!</u>

Keep your heart true, pure, but tender,
you must really always remember, true love
will always surrender, cause-
<u>LOVE WILL FIND THE WAY!</u>

By-Raymond Quattlebaum-AKA-Ray Q

<u>Friends</u>

True, precious, extremely dear.
People make diamonds,
friends are rare.
Diamonds glitter,
but friends care.
Like the love that's meant to share.
Wait a minute!
Am I hearing you clear,
true friends,
are always there.
Whatever the situation,
they don't disappear.
Are you feeling me from here!
How many survive without
their love and care.
No matter how you see it, they're there!
A toast to both of us, a celebration cheer.
An understanding so powerful,
you can't compare.
It becomes an overwhelming yeah!
Ascending like a spiral stair.
Yes! Diamonds are occasionally rare,
they even glitter crystal clear.
But true friends are not found everywhere.
However, they glitter just as clear,
so now you see them from over here!!!
Showing their love out of care.

By-Raymond Quattlebaum-AKA-Ray Q

God Got Your Back!

The Strength of The Universe.
The Power of Truth.
Dear God of Thunder,
please hold my hand,
there is evil in this land.
Should I be afraid because I did all I can.
Kill them with truth, you better take a stand,
I despise this darkness, that's not who I am.
Fight them off, show them the light,
their only weakness is what's right.
I hit'em with a right,
I hit'em with a left, hoping that they'll confess.
These forces of evil got me scared for sure.
The Devil of Darkness stands by the door.
These forces of evil God grow at night,
so fight them with eternal light.
He has no power who stands by the door,
God's the one, who loves you more!
I tried to explain how they're lost,
I even showed them the Holy Cross.
I said obey God, or bring it to order,
or I'll fight you with some Holy Water.
So you still wanna play, you have nothing to say,
then die your way. But remember the word
Judgement Day.
The truth is Truthfully the only way.
So, you become weak, when I start to pray.
Evil is what you love to display,
God's Truth is what I live for today.
Is there anything you wanna say?
You better look for a brighter day,
because God is definitely on his way!
And the Devil is the one he's going to slay.
Because God lives for a brighter day!!!
I specialize from above, my reality is Love.
I am The Light over Darkness.
I am The Strength of Power.
I grow Stronger hour by hour.
I am the Lightning in the Sky.
I am the reason why you Die.

I am The Creator of Creation.
I will Annihilate those in Damnation.
I am The Power of Creation.
Yes! I AM All That There Is To Be!
High in his Infinite Glory.
I am The One who tells a story.
I Am The Truth of Light.
I live for everything that's Right!
I Am God! HELLO!!!

By-Raymond Quattlebaum-AKA-Ray Q

Greatness!

You are not what you appear to be,
I am not what you appear to see.
We are a physical manifestation
of spirit in human form.

This is not my real face,
that is not your real face,
I am within you, you are within me.
I am you within me, spirit!

We are who we are within each other,
expressions of the soul, the real you.
We are a reflection of All That There Is To Be!
Spiritual beings experiencing physical reality.

Straight from the All Mighty himself,
a force to be reckon with.
Dancing in a sea of unconditional love.
We glide through an ocean of cosmic, ethereal, electromagnetic energy.

As we express ourselves through physical reality,
transforming ourselves in and out of various lives,
experiencing life in the flesh.
We go home every now and again as we die,

but we come back again when we're born.
A cycle of spiritual growth,
a learning experience.
Apparently, life is more than the physical transition.

Just as we go through a physical transition,
the soul goes through a spiritual one.
We are spiritual beings experiencing physical reality.
Not physical beings experiencing a spiritual one, we are the soul.

By-Raymond Quattlebaum-AKA-Ray Q 6/2/06

I Am

Who am I,
am I my thoughts,
or my feelings.
Or expressions of thoughts,
with feelings.
Maybe thoughts experiencing
feelings of expressions.
Maybe an entity
with collective feeling tones,
of what life should be.
Perhaps an individual,
facing a devastation of cold,
and knowledge the blanket of cover.
However, I am, who I am, therefore
everlasting I am.
The chapters of life,
here today, gone tomorrow.
But I must know who I am.
Am I the conscious, the subconscious,
the superconscious,
the past, the present, the future.
Who am I, I am who,
can I be, who I am.
The I, the me, the you, the self,
the will, the ego, the emotion,
the thought, the love.
Which one am I, can I be the all.
Therefore, believe it, or not,
I am evermore, forever more.
Basically which one are you,
take a guess?
Why I must be the battle in the sky.
The sky my mentality,
the battle what lies within.
Who am I, I am, who I am.
That's why I am,
in the beginning I am, therefore,
I will always be who I am.
I am who, I am.
I am all that, and even more, that's who I am.
I am forever!

By-Raymond Quattlebaum-AKA-Ray Q
9/22/01

I Am Love!

Out of all the miracles of love,
my love is beautiful.
I am forever love, the color of life,
I am loved forever.
everybody holds me, lets me go,
but always comes back for more.
I am irresistable.
Lurking in the shadows in the landscape
of your mind. Like the colors of a rainbow.
The star of happiness, stirring emotions
within your heart.
Yes, I love you, love!
Dancing in heavens glory of light.
Images of shooting stars at night. Yes I am love.
And all love is a reflection of who I am love.
And how I have grown through love to be loved.
Yes, I am love, holding you tight,
in the wee hours of the morning.
Tasting your everlasting love. The miracle of life.
the vision of a dream.
Like the colors of creation mesmerized magnificently.
Pretty love is the color of life.
Two hearts holding each other in the shadow of night.
ever so beautifully, as we bath in the corona of love.
Baby! I could never ignore you. I simple adore you.
for I am love, the flame of life.
burning in your heart.
Yes! Everlasting love I am.
spinning in a circle of wondrous joy. I am forever.
Like the circle of life.

I'll Be There!

Honey! don't stop the tears from falling on my
tear stain face. Beautifying the passion
within my soul, a love so deep.
Embrace my love. Honey! I will be there my love.
In the still of the night.
In the wee hours of the morning, unrecorded,
unseen, the spirit of love.
Baby I will be there forever.
And I will live in the vastness of your beauty forever.
In the sea of your wetness, forevermore.
Riding on the waves of our love, up and down,
back and forth, in and out.
Rejoicing in the movement of of our waterfalls, baby.
Loving every passing delectable minute.
Ecstasy, Passion, the delicious of love.
God's spiritual rain.
And I will feel this way forever.
Sensuous. Caressivness. Specializing. Appetizing.
All wrapped up into one, sweet love.
Darling by now you know this is how we come.
However, when the ship pulls in baby, i will be
looking for a taste of honey.
And I will love this way forever and forever.
In the confine of our love.
Angelic love. Heavenly love.
Baby it's love forevermore, your love, baby.
Provocative. Delectable. Absolutely. Remarkable.
Baby you are incrdible.
knowing in the morning blue,
my heavenly angel, baby you!!!
The heavenly things that we do, beautiful baby, me and you.
A love affair that's so true.
Angels are whispering about me and you.
And I will love this way forever and ever.
In the town of your beautiful mound, baby,
forever and forever and forevermore.
In the garden of love.
Baby it's our time, isn't it beautiful! The Color Of Love!!

It's Crazy!

Crazy, crazy,
the whole world
is going crazy.
Don't tell me,
it's crazy!
Your crazy, she's crazy,
the whole world is going crazy,
can't you see,
it's crazy!
No one sees, it's crazy.
THERE USE TO BE A TIME,
when you could spend
a quarter, or a dime,
had a nickel in your pocket,
and you still
was feeling fine.
BUT THE WORD THEY CALL INFLATION,
has taken away your
material shine.
It's enough to trigger your pockets,
at the same time blow your mind.
THERE USE TO BE A TIME,
when you could tell the people
what you know,
but the world has change so much,
you can't even say Hello!
That's why their crazy,
we're crazy,
the entire world's going crazy.
Don't you see!
It's crazy.
I'm crazy, he's crazy,
the world's going crazy, crazy, crazy.
Please! Won't you see!
It's crazy!
BUT IF WE ALL HOLD HANDS,
and try to help each
other out,
it would be heaven
here on earth,

is what the Angels song about.
But the world will look
at you, and say,
that joke was very funny,
cause the most important
things are Prestige,
Power, and Money.
Wooooooow! That's crazy!
How crazy, Toooo, Crazy!

Nations destroyed because of the love
that's meant to share.
People in high places see the destruction,
and don't even care.
Destruction like a spiral stair.
Wait a minute! Does anyone really care?
Can't we all just share.
That's why It's Crazy, It's Crazy,
I Can't believe life's so crazy.
1. 2. 3. It's crazy.,
can't somebody see, It's Crazy.
We're crazy, your crazy,
The whole world's going absolutely crazy.
But no one sees, It's Crazy!
If the world took time out to see,
that the best things in life are free.
We would put an end to problems,
that would never have to be.
We must come to an understanding,
that we are all the same.
We should all take the blame,
for calling people names.
We should all be ashamed,
for causing people pain.
What are we insane!
We better call God's name,
because life is not a game.
That's why she's crazy, your crazy, he"s crazy, I'm
crazy,
It's Crazy, crazy, crazy.

It's not for me, It's Crazy.
How crazy, real crazy.
And if you don't watch out,
You'll be crazy. Please! Wake up! And see! It's
Crazy.
And if you don't wanna see, then your real
Crazy!!!!
Believe me, now how could this be,
POW! POW! POW! It's Crazy!
Because no one wants to see, It's Crazy!!!!

By-Raymond Quattlebaum AKA- Ray Q

In The Belly Of The Beast

Remember the biblical
tale of Joanna,
who got swallowed by the whale,
forever deceased.
Locked up in the belly of the beast.
So you bust your gun,
I'll bust mine,
a thousand clips in the gat,
but the outcome is time.
When is all this destruction
ever gonna cease,
caught up in a time warp
in the belly of the beast.
Our lives revolve around negative
connotations,
the ghetto life has no limitations.
Fast lane life pushing
big expensive cars,
people selling drugs so they
can live large.
When is all this destruction
ever gonna cease,
time moves on in the belly of the beast.
The quality of ghetto life
seems like it never had a chance,
turn the music up this is why we dance.
Doing everything and anything
just to make a dollar,
killing people in the streets
makes me wanna halla!
When is all this destruction
ever gonna cease,
gotta keep it movin,
in the belly of the beast.
And when you make it out praying
never to fall back,
negative forces telling you
this is where it's at.
Making power moves
to make sure you don't fail,

because in all reality
your done off in jail.
Aw! Man! This ain't even good,
just another day of sorrow
living in the hood.
Lost in a ball of confusion
with no place to go, hold that thought!
If you never been to the ghetto,
you just don't know.
When is all this destruction
ever gonna cease!
This is what the bible talks
about in the belly of the
beast!

By-Raymond Quattlebaum-
AKA-Ray Q

I wonder!

Do you ever wonder?
Where does a thought go,
when it leaves your mind.
I wonder?

Do you ever wonder?
What makes you wonder!
Why you wonder, what you wonder,
when you wonder, as you wonder,
in wonder.

In the colors .of your mind,
happiness in your heart,
beauty of your soul.
Do you ever wonder?

As you wonder, in your wonder,
life's a wonder, within a wonder,
so you wonder, with a wonder.

Because you wonder, in your wonder,
should you wonder, not to wonder,
ever wonder, cause you wonder,
why you wonder, with a wonder.
Maybe you wonder? What you wonder,

while you wonder, it takes a wonder,
to make you wonder. What you wonder,
as you wonder, in your wonder, with a wonder.
In the memories of your mind, minutes of time,

moments of silence.
Do you really ever wonder?
What you wonder, when you wonder,
life's a wonder, how do we wonder?
What we wonder, makes you wonder, how you
wonder.

So we wonder, this wonder, we wonder,
in wonder, no wonder, I wonder, with wonder.
And all the time you wonder.

wonder, and wonder, so much wonder,
in wonder. Do you ever wonder?
Never wonder, while you wonder,
as you wonder, when you wonder,

not to wonder, what you wonder,
in your wonder, with a wonder.
Perhaps, you don't even wonder?
You just speculate, so why wonder!

By-Raymond Quattlebaum-A.K.A.-Ray Q

Just My Imagination

Your love is soft, sweet, music,
playing in heaven's morning blue.
Am I dreaming, or is this true!
As I turned around I envision you my dear,

clouds of love sprinkled everywhere.
You are singing on heaven's glass stair,
this vision of you is crystal clear.
Your body shaped like an angelic pear,

twilights of music fill the air,
sounds of trumpets blowing everywhere.
Could it be I'm really here, oh! My dear!
An array of colors, oh! Look over there,

heavenly bodies seem to appear,
baby angels stand up and cheer.
Love's desperation has brought us here,
embrace me with both hands my darling dear.

Is there something you wanna share,
there's no reason for us to fear.
God is watching from a tier,
angels are dancing on a sphere.

Who is it, who said life isn't fair,
would you prefer candle light dinner for two my
dear,
Angel's Cuisine is right over there.
The man playing music across from here,

I have some dollars I can spare.
They're playing our song my darling dear,
the smell of love is in the air.
Now the picture is crystal clear,

so let me nibble on your ear,
but there are people sitting everywhere.
Darling my love for you I do not care,
because I will love you anywhere.

Then an audience of people clapped and cheered,
in just one minute it all disappeared.
Why it was just my imagination,
aw! Dreams are not fair!

By-Raymond Quattlebaum-AKA-Ray Q

23

Keep Me Coming
Baby!
Keep Me Coming Back For More!

two hearts in love
mean that much more.
Romantic evenings we both adore.
Candle light dinner,
make love on the floor.

KEEP ME COMING BACK FOR MORE!

Take long strolls together
through the park,
keep it movin in the dark.
Have a glass of some chill wine,
baby I massage your body,
you massage mine.

KEEP ME COMING BACK FOR MORE!

Make love by the fire place,
baby we don't have no time to waste.
It's a Romantic Delicious space,
baby! It's your body I wanna taste.
Darling watch the expression on
your face.

KEEP ME COMING BACK FOR MORE!

I take off your clothes,
you take off mine,
baby I'm about to blow your mind.
Lets not even consider the time,
someone so beautiful and so fine,
magnificent love is on my mind.

KEEP ME COMING BACK FOR MORE!

Love, this is our chance to be alone,
baby it's a pleasure to hear you moan.

Because your sexy and your grown,
I'm about to reach my Throne.
Who did you say was on the phone?

<u>KEEP ME COMING BACK FOR MORE</u>!

I love you, and you love me, baby
beautiful love is suppose to be,
the essence of love is unbelievably
free. We are the essence baby, you
and me. Incredible love, Atmospheric
free!!!

<u>KEEP ME COMING BACK FOR MORE</u>!

And more, and more, and more, baby!
Keep me coming back for more, and
forevermore, more, your more.

Yes! Baby! Keep Me Coming!!!!!!!

"Listen"

This Is Something That We Rate
Real Things In Life That Are Great

The joy of love which flows through our heart,
beautiful colors we call art. The sky, the-
birds and the trees, the insects, the pollen,
the nectar and bees.

This Is Something That We Rate
Real Things In Life That Are Great

The rainbow, the ocean, and the sun, this is
how you know there's only one.
The different colors of the races, other
directions we call places. The air, the weather,
the color of green, fish in their world we call
marine.

This Is Something That We Rate
Real Things In Life That Are Great

The planets, the stars and the ground, this is
how it comes around. Male, female and their off-
spring, we come together to do our thing.
The hugging, the kissing, the way we feel,
this is how you know it's for real.

This Is Something That We Rate
Real Things In Life That Are Great

The beauty of life goes so far, the essence of
life are who we are. The forces in life that
represent you, and all the things we dream about
that's just so true. You wouldn't be life
if life wasn't you.

This Is Something That We Rate
Real Things In Life That Are Great!

By-Raymond Quattlebaum AKA-Ray Q

Look At You!

A light shines within your being.
Though we do all our thinking
with the infinite mind.
There are levels within reality,
we all must climb.
When you channel positive energy
you begin to shine.
Like an artist paints a picture,
the composite is time.
Now individuals who lack the under-
standing of the situation they're in,
fail to realize we are born to win.
Trumpets are played from the day you're born,
the purpose of life is to move on.
There are Angels all around you,
who're singing this song.
Because you made it through birth,
you must be strong.
The magnificence of life must go on.
I made you from the strongest material there
could ever be, this is why you are made in the image of me.

Life is the miracle we all must see,
your human reality was born to be free!
This corporeal reality will never stand still,
because humanity was born with infinite free will.
Understand the greatness of your bill,
you have the Power and Strength to tackle any hill.
So when you feel down, and can't go on,
just remember this saying, you must be Strong!!!

By-Raymond Quattlebaum-AKA-Ray Q

Part-1

Dedicated
To
My Mother!

Master Of The Ring

One of our Legendary Greats
has passed on, a Loved Angel.
Loved by all those who've
felt the love within her heart.
She's called:

A Diamond. A Ruby. A Sapphire.
An Emerald. A Pearl. Black Onyx.
Tripple Platinum.
Treasure Of All Treasures.
A Queen Jewel.
A Black African Queen.

In this corner we have Mrs. Mavis Quattlebaum
fighting The Ring Of Life.
In the other corner we have The Ring Of Life.
I want you both to shake hands and come out fighting.
One who sits on a Throne, but not alone.
She holds the title for any bout fight.
Heavy-Weight Champion Of The World, I presume.
A. K. A. The Hammer!
She's known to knockout responsibilities with her bare hands.
A True Master!
I had to raise five kids all by myself.
I never said life wasn't hard.
For most people are afraid of the ring.
She's the best dancer I have ever seen.
She's known to knockout responsibilities
with multiple combinations.
Her secret to life is stick and move.
When a situation becomes too tough, she bobs and weave.
But when she's backed up into a corner,

she comes out swinging.
And when it becomes too intense, she starts to dance.
And if she's too tired, she uses The Rope A Dope.
For most men are known to take their hats off to her.
Her record is so outstanding there's no room for talk.
The Ring Of Life threw a series of combinations and a left hook.
But my mother bobed and weaved, then she started to dance.

As my mother knocked out The Ring Of Life,
for a few seconds, only to find out.
No matter how many times she hit The Ring Of Life
he wouldn't stay down, he just kept on coming.
Because The Ring Of Life can't be destroyed,
it's a life time ring. You See! there's a Ring Of Life
we all must fight, A.K.A.
The Ring Of Responsibilities.
I fight because The Ring Of Life is everybody's fight,
no one can walk away, because your life is The Ring.
For she has an Entourage Of Professional Women Fighters
known to come together, from all around the world,
in all life situations, called W.H. I. D. A.
Known as Women Hold It Down Association.
Who raise their kids all by themselves.
She has been fighting for me ever since I was born,
and every other life situation after.
There is no one more sweeter and deserves the name Sugar
in the ring, than my Dear old Sweet Mother.
If there's another word that describes the word Beautiful,
it would be my Mother, deep within her heart.
Her memory will live on forever, her fight will live on
through us all. We Love you Mom with all our heart and soul.
With every fiber of our being. You are the music in our lives.
We are going to miss you Mom, Dearly.
You are the Greatest Mother in the world.
You are a True Master Mom!
Master Of The Ring! Mom, True, Love!!!
No one never really dies,
it's just a transition to another state of consciousness.
Energy can't be destroyed, it could only be changed
into another form of matter.
The spirit lives on forever outside the human body.
Yes! Life goes on!!!

By-Raymond Quattlebaum AKA. Ray Q

Poetry In Motion

Have you ever seen art
drawn on ice,
the element of surprise,
it's unbelievably nice.
A beautiful picture that's
worth the price,
professional skaters who
dance on ice.
No matter how you see it
take my advice,
all the money in the world
it's worth the price.
Moves that are made to blow your mind,
why these people can stop
right on a dime.
Believe it, or not,
they got perfect time,
like diamonds on ice how
they glitter and shine.
The moves that make,
awe! they're just that great,
jumps in the air a figure 8.
What a picture! It's drawn so nice,
watching them skate and dance on ice.
The way they move with so much pride,
a skip, a jump, within a glide.
Beautiful music becomes the place,
how they specialize with rythm,
style, a dance of grace.
As they move the looks on their face,
thousands of people surround the place.
A beautiful picture displayed on ice,
professional skaters known as nice.
Acrobatic acts, jumps in the air,
thousands of people stand up and cheer,
interested people from everywhere.
Because they skate with so much pride,
it's a thrill to see them glide.
It's almost like they got a ride,
a skip, a jump, within a glide.
Why it makes me wish I was on their side,
how they skate with so much pride!!!

<u>Sadness</u>

<u>Can You See The Sadness?</u>

That's destroying this beautiful world.

<u>Can You See The Sadness?</u>

In the eyes of boys and girls.

<u>Can You See The Sadness?</u>

That life is just a dream, and all the things you think about may not be what they seem.

<u>Can You See The Sadness?</u>

That we all one day sure will die.

<u>Can You See The Sadness?</u>

Without someone starting to cry.

<u>Can You See The Sadness?</u>

In the way some people think, and if we don't do something about it, our reality will start to sink.

<u>Can You See The Sadness?</u>

It's a ball of share utter confusion.

<u>Can You See The Sadness?</u>

That life is just a mere illusion.

<u>Can You See The Sadness?</u>

That the world is filled with drugs, and
no matter how we see it, our children should
be hugged.

Can You See The Sadness?

Because we all have a dream, and no matter how
we see it, life is what it seems.

Can You See The Sadness?

By-Raymond Quattlebaum-AKA-Ray Q

The Ball Of Confusion
9/11

On that dreadful day, the greatest nation
in the world was out to play,
why a terrible evil has got in our way.
Destroy this great nation that stands today,
and anybody else who had anything to say,
a black plaque became that day.
Thousands of lives please! Why this way!
A terrorist attack started it all,
the element of surprise made it fall.
The majority of times we're on our guard,
a destruction this big we took it hard.
Who would ever think an evil lurked within,
in all reality they could never win.
A devastating tragedy, how it blew our mind's,
the destruction of all, and the World's Skyline.
Thousands of thousands of victims afraid,
the anihilation, the World's Trade.
Who is responsible for the ignorance that pervade,
believe it, or not, a terrorist crusade.
A terrible evil, without feelings, it's not right,
<u>King Prince Of Darkness</u>, the devil in the light.
Rescue workers from all walks of life,
came to save us, and you know that ain't right.
Everyday people doing what they got to do,
they anihilated their lives, and we felt it too!
Innocent victims who had to die, you can't tell me
you didn't cry! No time today, needless to say,
we'll build it back up a Memorial Day.
A senseless crime, a cowardly act, no element of
surprise, we'll get you back.
Now any other time we would never stand still, but
this one time we had to chill.
A ball of confusion, a dark night, a mystery, this
will always be front page history.
When will they realize that's not where it's at,
going around killing people with terrorist attacks.
Now this is far beyond any stormy weather,
it took a tragedy like this, to bring us all together.

By-Raymond Quattlebaum-AKA-Ray Q 9/20/01

The Beautiful Black Woman

Out of all the treasures in the world,
comes a true hidden treasure.
The Majesty of her <u>BLACKNESS</u>, <u>BLACK-EBONY</u>,
<u>MAHOGANY-BEAUTY</u>, <u>BLACK-ONYX</u>.
She is life's persue of happiness and strength.
There are no women more dazzling, more powerful,
than a beautiful blackwoman.
She is truly Mother Of Civilization,
the birth-right of all human life.
There is nothing more beautiful in vision,
and forever like her to see.
And all female denominations are a reflection
of who she is, all females.
She is truly one of a kind, and forever no more.
Who can bear her life line tittle:

1-The way she walks.
2-The way she talks.
3-The look in her eyes.
4-The beauty of her smile.
5-Her luscious full lips.
6-Her voluptuous beautiful breasts.
7-Her devastating unbelievable body.
8-The way she moves.
9-The way she grooves.
10-The electricity in her hair.
11-The warmth of her touch.
12-The awesome color of her skin.
13-Her outstanding, breathtaking shine.
14-Her intelligent mind.
15-She is really absolutely fine.
16-Baby it's love all the time.

May I say more! Your Highness.
She radiates in a fashion so profound,
one only begs to see.
Who could ever resist her pretty,
in obsession to her beauty.
May I color you beautiful your Highness,
in contrast to all colors your Majesty.
Your such a Queen. Blackwoman, your such a prize.
A comfort in my heart for all times.
Queen, of Queens, your Majesty, your Highness.
I must never let you go.
You breathe life into all life,
and the world becomes free. I say your horizon is my future. Other's say, your my destiny to behold.
For I will be with her until time passes over, and life begins again. She is the Alpha and the Omega. There would never be a time when you wouldn't
hear these four beautiful, magnificent, words.
<u>The</u> <u>Beautiful</u> <u>Black</u> <u>Woman</u>. Baby it's <u>love</u>, until <u>death</u>
due us both apart. Baby I will long for you, until hell freezes over, and life becomes living again. Forever would never be never, my love, is your love, my love, baby, forever!

By-Raymond Quattlebaum-AKA-Ray Q

The Incredible Inevitable!

Lets take a look at life,
a spiritual advice.
Our gift from God is true,
the power lies in you.
What you do with your life
is your gift to God,
the road life is hard.
There's no escaping God,
because we all punch a card.
For you see God before your born,
as life struggles on,
and after you die,
what an incredible high.
No matter how you try,
this is why we cry,
it's Heaven in your eyes.
For Man has free will,
but animals have to kill.
Man must be a Man,
his life is in demand.
With his Darling wife Woman,
the other side of Man,
life is more than grand,
because God is in command.
We are all Divine,
God's consciousness incline.
It's called the Infinite Mind.
However, some may find this hard,
but we have the nature of God.
Now understand why we are great,
we have the power to create.
So understand why we're born,
the meaning of life is Strong,
it's Strength to carry on.
He says we are all God's
not the Supreme Being Of
All That There Is To Be!
But his offsprings that are
free. Life is a beautiful
gift, cherish her wisely or

she can shift.
You can be anything you want
to be, now you understand
why life is free.
Keep your mind and body in
good shape, God says it's
never too late.
We all have Godly skills,
you can change your mind at
will. This is why life is
free, you create your re-
ality. And anything you do,
your life represents you.
Take a look at who you are,
you have the propensity of a
Star! Male and Female must
prevail, somethings in life
are not for sale, not on
any scale.
Humanity has a higher rea-
lization, for he is Crown Of
Creation. With the Know-
ledge and Power to build a
nation. What a beautiful in-
clination, yes, with Pride
and Determination.

By-Raymond Quattlebaum-AKA-Ray Q

The Rythm
Of
Love!

Love! Arrows of happiness, while some say,
mixtures of pain.
Some lack the understanding,
while some feel it's spiritual rain.
Who am I to dance with no rythm in my heart,
I can't find my way, I'm lurking in the dark.
It's a mystery of horror, no a dungeon of fear.
I can't shake this feeling,
a terror grows near.
What a lonely feeling, please!
love me my dear! In it's darkest hour,
a vision appears.
Angelic beings with knowledge in mind,
no rythm in your heart is a clock out of time.
Here's an implication of what love should be,
take it from an Angel, true love is free.
Drink this magic potion, and try it again,
message on the bottle love starts within.
It dissipated the feeling, my love started to shine,
I felt Love and Understanding, I started feeling fine,
What's this magic potion a secret, an art,
I got on the floor, I felt rythm in my heart.
In it's darkest hour, true love started to start.
When you have no rythm, you can't even dance,
what about a little, not even a chance.
Love has many chapters a Beginning and an End,
but the greatest of them all is The Love that's within.
Stop! And think about it!
Is there anyone out there listening!
Let me give it to you again!!!!

Keep Your Head To The Sky!

When your down and feeling low, and family
are telling you absolutely no!
Because you have no place to go.

Keep Your Head To The Sky!

lost your job, down and out, destruction seems to
come about, without a shadow of a doubt,
don't let misery turn you out. This is not your final route.
Your faith in destiny will come about.

Keep Your Head To The Sky!

You aim to get it right again, but there's no real
help from your friends, And time seems to pass you by,
you scratch your head and wonder why!

Keep Your Head To The Sky!

You must battle the good with the bad,
sometimes life can make you sad, especially if you lost
everything you had, these realities will make you mad.
But life goes on, so still be glad. Life won't always be that bad

Keep Your Head To The Sky!

If you give up on life for who you are,
you will only go so far.
What about the concept of who you are, self belief will
take you far. Show them the concept of who you are.
You are the offspring of a star, this is the power of who you are
The battle in life will take you far.
Know the power of who you are, it's your strength that will
take you far

Keep Your Head To The Sky!

You Are Love!

The Beholder of all Beauty.
You are the Twinkle in my eye.
The Story of my life.
You are Heaven in the Flesh.
I fall apart,
when we don't come together.
Forever hold me,
I am yours to behold.
Love! How I hunger for your love.
Love! You are the Castle in my Sky,
all your love tells me why.
Love! My heart bleeds for you.
I could spin around in a twirl,
because I know you are my world.
Love! Not only are you the real thing,
your voice of love makes Heaven sing.
Love! When I kiss you love,
and hold you tight,
your ecstasy of love sends me in flight.
Love! You are more than just a dream,
you're an Angel on the seen.
You're the topping on Ice Cream,
and everything else in between.
Love! Dear, Love, when I think about
you night and day,
you just take my breath away.
A lost for words I could definitely say.
Your Love's the power of today,
God has sent you here to stay.
Heaven is what love will say,
Beauty is Love on it's way.
There is nothing for me to fear.
Love! You will always be my Dear,
in my heart I love you Clear.
Your love is written everywhere!
Yes! Love is something that you share,
I won't let you disappear.
You are Love!!!

By-Raymond Quattlebaum AKA-RayQ

You Can't See Me

Born from the essence,
created by God.
Other people telling me
my nature is a fraud.

<u>You Can't See Me!</u>

I was here first, time,
circulates fast.
Fairy Tales and Myths,
don't never last. Here today,
destroyed by sorrow.
Open the history books it
dictates tomorrow.

<u>You Can't See Me!</u>

I'm the strength color of
all races, look around the world,
relics in all places.

<u>You Can't See Me!</u>

They colored the world, now how
could this be, this is why you
can't see me. No one's perfect,
we all make mistakes,
then tell them the truth for
heaven sake.

<u>You Can't See Me!</u>

What you gave out, you'll
get back, secrets of the universe
telling me that's a fact.
I'm not that race depicted as low,
telling the truth we all will grow.

<u>You Can't See Me!</u>

Destroy that lie, toss it up in the air,
because we do care.
The truth is something that won't
disappear. <u>Guardians of Justice</u>.
<u>Custodians of Peace</u>.
This is what you'll find
on our spiritual lease.

<u>You Can't See Me!</u>

I am an excellent
practioner in the art
that is mine,
and my conversation is
the superiority of my
intelligent mind.
The truth is the light
we're bound to find.

<u>You Can't See Me!</u>

Because you don't see
me, for who I am
Historically!
I am the Darker Brother
I've been blinded by
the whie light, my
whole entire life.
You mean to tell me,
You can't see me!
I am the Darker
Brother!
You Can't See Me!!!

By-Raymond Quattlebaum
AKA-Ray Q

39

Your Love!

Your love is a camp fire,
burning in the night.
I add my wood to your fire,
to make the flames ignite.
It's such a beautiful atmosphere,
the scenery so bright. Holding
my baby love, so dear, our reflection
in the light.
Loving you is what I do baby, a beauty
so right. There's nothing I wouldn't
do my dear, to keep our love tight.
Our bodies rubbing close together,
friction in the night. The fire burning
in our hearts, like a burning light.
And all the while I'm loving you, a
sexual appetite. Wolves are howling
look my dear, isn't that a sight!
Shooting stars throughout the air,
this is some delight.
I visualize me a King on a Throne,
my baby all dressed in White,
you are a Heavenly Light.
Baby you are right, love is a beautiful sight.
Heaven is love on a Throne making love at night.
Beautiful, baby, our love's a storybook dream,
what a celestial scene.
Baby you are the Icing, honey I am the Cream.
Yes, My, Love, Heaven is as beautiful as it seems.
Real love, baby, do you know what I mean.
We are a Romantic Team.
Baby you are a Angelic Queen.
Yes! Honey! Heaven is what we seen,
our love is not a dream.
It taste like Peaches And Cream,
your love makes me wanna scream!!!!
This is what Heaven is all about, when Love is on the scene!

By-Raymond Quattlebaum-AKA-Ray Q

Who Am I

When I am you, and you am I.

Who Am I

When darkness has surrounded me, and there is no light.

Who Am I

If love has broken me down, and there is no one to behold.

Who Am I

If living is dying and life is to live.

Who Am I

When you don't even know yourself, but yourself knows who you are.

Who Am I

If I am lost in a crowd, and no one knows my name.

Who Am I

You are who you are, but do you know, who you are. No!

Who Am I

They say what you think is who you are, but if I don't think, then who am I.

Who Am I

In a doggie dogged world, where big fish
eat little fish, and I'm just somebody
elses prey.

Who Am I

They say no one can ride your back unless
it's bend, you are who you are because
you say you are, that's who you are.

Who Am I

Know thy self, know who you are.
I am knowledge. Know-ledge, if you know
the ledge, you won't fall off.

I Am knowledge, the essence of life, the strength of power.
Universal mind. I Am everything.

Knowledge is Who I Am. I Am knowledge.
You must Know The ledge, because you won't fall off.

Knowledge is the Power of strength!
The Power of Life. They call it the ledge.

Knowledge!!! Because you won't fall off.
It is The Strength Of Life!!!

By-Raymond Quattlebaum AKA- Ray Q

<u>What Is Love?</u>

The expression of freedom,
an emotion unseen,
a figment of imagination,
am I living a dream.
The blossoms of roses
as I lay in my bed,
up and down feelings,
love plays with your head.
A beautiful feeling,
the color of red.
Those without feelings are usually dead.
You can't touch an emotion,
but color a thought,
love is something that can't be bought.
Future reservations play in your mind,
distorted visions love is blind.
A display of honey, attracted by bees,
the nectar, the pollen,
the color of trees.
The smell of evergreen, the sun that shines,
the beauty of living in this day and time.
The Waterfalls, the Ocean,
the reflection of Stars,
Jupiter, Venus, Pluto, and Mars.
When two sexes come together
to do their thing,
the ultimate achievement is what the future brings.
The beauty of a baby being born,
or the propagation of life moving on.
The beautiful feelings we feel in our heart,
we put it on paper and call it art.
The greatest manifestation of all life in existence,
when it comes to love there is no resistance.
An impeccable beauty, when we do our thing.
The prettiest of all feelings,
this is why we sing! What Is Love?

By-Raymond Quattlebaum-AKA-Ray Q

Black People

Whatever happened to Ebony,
Mocha, Mahogany, Chocolate,
Black Onyx.
Black people, there use to be
a time, when we was who we was.
But somewhere in history,
our knowledge has gotten lost.
Why, we are not these same
people today, stolen legacy is
what we say.
They take credit for things
they did not do,
now this confuses me and you.
We are the history they
claim to be,
hiding the truth from you and me.
Primitive savages
is what we are called,
we're God's righteous people
who have started it all.
We've been broken down in color
to Morning, Afternoon, Evening
and Night,
a ball of confusion dosen't
make it right.
We are responsible for beautiful things,
the dynasty roll of Black Queens & Kings.
The majority of our youth
don't know jack,
we must fight for who we are,
and you know that's a fact.
They step on us like we are the ground,
we can't keep going through life
being put down.
There was a time when black was
the height strength of a nation,
where's our pride and determination.
We must claim all that we are,
that's the only way to get far.
They lie to you and say your

nothing but slaves, open your heart,
it's time to be brave.
We had powers that others
couldn't understand,
now this same power god gave to man.
What was pure and natural is no more,
this is why we should've closed our door.
We live in a world of all sorts
of pollution, the external
reality is all an illusion.
A people who made us No.1
rejection, this world is build
on lies and deception.
We must build our own world,
that represents us, and rise
again, from dawn to dusk.
The hearts of those of us who
love our people bleed. It cuts
like a knife.
My people go with God. One
with god is a majority. If god
be on our side, who can be against
us.

By-Raymond Quattlebaum-AKA-Ray Question

Printed in the United States
By Bookmasters